# Undiscovered France

On the eastern slopes of the Massif, the road from the Rhône valley winds past banks planted with vines and fruit trees to reach the small valley of the river Couzon. In a detour along a sunken lane is the entrance gate of an old charterhouse. When the Carthusian monks built Sainte-Croix-en-Jarez, little did they know that, after the French Revolution, the farmers and artisans of the region would buy the whole monastery to turn it into the unusual village that it is today.

The village has no street, only two large courtyards linked by a long vaulted passageway.

A few rooms of the old priory – the old kitchen, the library and the abbot's room – have been turned into a museum. But the official structure of a French village is all there: the church, the *mairie*, a restaurant, and village houses with little gardens, once cultivated by monks. Life here still seems to be spent in almost monkish self-sufficiency.

Seen from the gardens of its château, the circular medieval village of Saint-Saturnin on the edge of France's volcanic heartland, looks like the perfect setting for a play: red-roofed houses surround the square, a fountain at its

*Charroux is a village famous for its stone quarries. Throughout the village are examples of the work of local stonemasons, from handsome doorways to small paved court-yards and the amazingly narrow pavements.*

*In Vogüé* (above), *as in many places along the Ardèche, canoeing is a popular summer recreation. Further up, in the river's deep gorges, there are excellent opportunities for white-water rafting and rock climbing.*

*Balazuc's cliff-top perch* (opposite) *is now appreciated by artists and artisans, rather than battle-scarred Saracens, but its ancient vaulted passageways* (right), *all sun and shadows, have changed little since medieval times.*

Travelling east, below Mont Gerbier-des-Joncs, source of the river Loire, the southern waters of the Ardèche flow past villages which begin to take on a Mediterranean feel. Vogüé, cradle of the most illustrious family of the Vivarais, les Seigneurs de Vogüé, is squeezed between the foot of a cliff and a loop in the river. Village and château have been built out of the same golden limestone and this and the round Roman tiles which cover the roofs give a distinctly southern look to the village.

This region of the Ardèche holds a surprising number of fortified hilltop villages, like the nearby feudal village of Rochecolombe. For a long time the area was racked by war and in 1427 the Vivarais was badly looted. A great number of villages also still carry the scars of the later conflicts of the Wars of Religion.

If, in Vogüé, only vestiges of the fortifications remain, the concern for defence can be seen in the way the tall, narrow houses have been built in relation to each other. To walk through the maze of streets and the complex series of vaulted passages is to understand how easily they could be both traps to the enemy and hidden escape routes.

The village is dominated by the four towers and stout walls of the imposing château. In the courtyard, the chapel displays treasures saved from the Rochecolombe church, and from the terraced gardens it is easy to imagine this ancient village little changed in the span of five hundred years.

It is believed that the Saracens settled in Balazuc in the eighth century. Certainly, the village, perched on the top of the cliff overlooking the river Ardèche, would have made a good watchpoint in belligerent times. Built around a thirteenth-century château and a Romanesque church, Balazuc is very characteristic of the region, built in light limestone and soft pink rounded tiles, *tuiles canas*. Modest tallish houses are linked by a supporting stone arch, creating a network of shaded walks through the village streets. If, at first, the houses had been built for defence, after the eighteenth century, when people found peace, the typical pattern of country life established itself here: the ground floor, often vaulted, was used as barn to keep sheep and goats and the upper floor was the living room.